Lin...

discover li...

D0513558

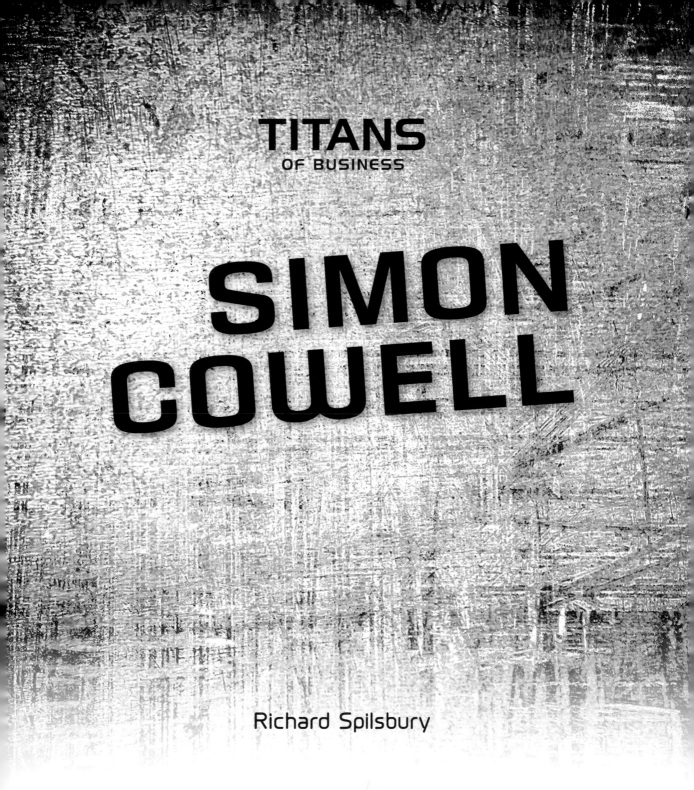

TITANS
OF BUSINESS

SIMON COWELL

Richard Spilsbury

Raintree

www.raintreepublishers.co.uk
Visit our website to find out more information about Raintree books.

To order:
☎ Phone 0845 6044371
🖹 Fax +44 (0) 1865 312263
🖳 Email myorders@raintreepublishers.co.uk

Customers from outside the UK please telephone +44 1865 312262

Raintree is an imprint of Capstone Global Library Limited, a company incorporated in England and Wales having its registered office at 7 Pilgrim Street, London, EC4V 6LB – Registered company number: 6695582

Edited by Mark Friedman, Nancy Dickmann, and Claire Throp
Designed by Richard Parker
Picture research by Liz Alexander
Original Illustrations © Capstone Global Library Ltd 2013
Illustrations by Darren Lingard
Originated by Capstone Global Library Ltd
Printed and bound in China by CTPS

ISBN 978 1 406 24035 1 (hardback)
16 15 14 13 12
10 9 8 7 6 5 4 3 2 1

British Library Cataloguing in Publication Data
Spilsbury, Richard, 1963-
Simon Cowell. -- (Titans of business)
791.4'5'092-dc23
A full catalogue record for this book is available from the British Library.

Acknowledgements
We would like to thank the following for permission to reproduce photographs: Alamy pp. 5 (© Trinity Mirror/Mirrorpix), 11 (© Marc Tielemans), 16 (© AF archive); Corbis pp. 31 (© Adam Knott/Corbis Outline), 39 (© Martin Roe/Retna Ltd); Getty Images pp. 18 (Steve Finn), 19 (Ray Mickshaw/WireImage), 21 (Mark Allan/WireImage), 23 (M Becker/American Idol 2009/Getty Images for Fox), 26 (Stefan Menne), 29 (James Sullivan/FilmMagic), 41 (Dave Hogan), 43 (Jordan Strauss/FilmMagic); Press Association Images pp. 22 (AP Photo/Times-News, Julie Basile), 30 (Andy Butterton/PA Archive), 33 (Elizabeth Pantaleo/ABACA USA/Empics Entertainment), 36 (Austin Hargrave/AP), 37 (John Stillwell/PA Archive); Rex Features p. 9 (ITV), 12 (Graham Troti/Daily Mail), 13 (William Lovelace/Daily Mail), 14 (MCP), 17 (Brian Rasic), 25 (Ken McKay), 34 (Matt Baron/BEI); Shutterstock p. 7 (© Patrick Hayes); ZUMA Press/Newscom p. 6.

Cover photograph reproduced with permission of Rex Features/Startraks Photo (main image) and Shutterstock/© Eky Studio (background image).

Every effort has been made to contact copyright holders of any material reproduced in this book. Any omissions will be rectified in subsequent printings if notice is given to the publisher.

Disclaimer

Contents

Find out what you need to do to have a successful career like Simon Cowell.

Read what Simon Cowell has said or what has been said about him.

Learn more about the people who influenced Simon Cowell.

Discover more about businesses that have been important during Simon Cowell's career.

Words printed in **bold** are explained in the glossary.

Introducing Simon Cowell

It is the final night of *The X Factor* and millions of television viewers are watching to find out who will win. There have been weeks of **media** coverage of the unfolding drama of the competition.

But whoever wins, the real victor is Simon Cowell. He invented and popularized this programme. When people phone in to vote for winners, or buy the records of the performers from the programme, Cowell and his businesses get paid enormous sums of money. This is not a one-off – Cowell has been responsible for many successful television programmes and music acts.

Famous entrepreneur

Cowell is one of the world's most famous **entrepreneurs** in the entertainment industry. Entrepreneurs are people who set up and run their own businesses. What makes them different from other business people is that they very often take big financial risks in order to take advantage of an opportunity to create and sell **products**.

Cowell's businesses include the television company that produces his hit talent shows *The X Factor*, *American Idol*, and *Britain's Got Talent*. His music companies have been discovering talent and producing hits since the early 1990s. He is a television personality himself, mostly as a judge on his own programmes, who appeals to wide audiences and attracts lots of **publicity**.

How did Simon Cowell become a titan of business? What risks and choices did he take and make along the way? Can we learn from his story so that we might succeed in business, too?

"The man who basically owns pop culture..."
Jemima Lewis, *The Telegraph*

> "Few have ever possessed such an **intuitive** understanding of the business of entertainment."
>
> Peter Aspden, *Financial Times*, 2010

Simon Cowell is one of the most powerful people in the global entertainment industry. Because his businesses have always made lots of money, Cowell's ideas and opinions about popular entertainment are taken very seriously.

The young Cowell

Simon Phillip Cowell was born in Brighton, on 7 October 1959. Simon was the first child of Julie and Eric. Between them, Julie and Eric had four children from previous marriages: John, Michael, Tony, and June. After Simon, Julie and Eric had two further children - brother Nicholas and sister Lindsay.

Simon was part of a family with strong showbusiness and media connections. Julie Cowell started dancing at the age of four and became a professional ballet dancer. Eric Cowell worked for EMI's property division.

Simon Cowell (left) with his brother. Simon and his brothers and sisters were often looked after by **nannies** because their parents were busy socializing.

Eric's job was well paid and the Cowells lived in a large house in the **suburbs** of Radlett, Hertfordshire. The family could afford to go on several foreign holidays a year – for example, to Bermuda in the West Indies.

Mixing with the stars

The Cowell family lived in quite a wealthy neighbourhood where many rich **executives** and film stars lived who worked at nearby **film studios** and record companies. The Cowells' neighbour worked for Warner Brothers film studios, This meant Simon had the chance to watch glamorous film stars, such as Elizabeth Taylor, enjoying parties over the garden fence. He later said: "I can remember it so well. They were larger-than-life, attractive, happy. I thought, 'This is very glamorous. I'd love to live in a house like that and have a party like that.'"

Bermuda was one of the places that the Cowell family went on holiday.

In trouble

Simon was often in trouble as a child and as a teenager. He was bored by lessons and hated the rules and discipline at school. He pretended to be ill, told teachers they were wasting their time, and played up. Not surprisingly his behaviour often got him into trouble, and he and his brother Nicholas were transferred to 16 different private schools as a result.

Simon was a handful at home, too. He once shaved his brother's hair off and he started to smoke. When he was 15, he drove his parents' car without permission and crashed it, luckily escaping injury. Julie tried to discipline Simon and he constantly argued with her, while Eric stayed out of it. Simon left school aged 16 with few good exam grades.

Getting to work

Fortunately Simon's parents had taught him the importance of hard work to earn your own money – even though they lived a luxurious lifestyle. Simon tried many holiday jobs as a teenager. He worked on a farm, washed cars, and mowed lawns. After Simon left school, Eric found him a job in the EMI postroom, sorting and delivering the post to different departments in the company. This was his first taste of the music industry.

> "He was a complete handful. Into everything... and he would not take 'no' for an answer. Then again, neither would I. It was a battle of wills."
>
> Julie Cowell, Simon's mother

Cowell and his mother are seen here at the recording of 2007's *This Is Your Life* television programme.

The music industry

From his first day in the postroom at EMI, Cowell began planning how to get to the top. He watched and learned all he could about the business and got to know people in the company. In 1979, he got his first break and was promoted to assistant to one of the executives.

The next step up the ladder was when Cowell got his first job as a music **producer**. His job was to discover the next big-selling stars, and to select the songs that could become their hits. It was not as glamorous as it sounds. His first office was a converted toilet in a central London car park! He later said: "In many ways, I was glad that I had started my career on the very low rung of the business. It was there that I learned how to deal with people."

As a music producer at EMI it was also Cowell's job to promote new acts. Promoting a new act means making it famous, by coming up with ideas to get singers on television or radio, and finding ways to make a band stand out from the crowd. Cowell soon showed a talent for promotion. Once he appeared on *Top of the Pops*, a television live music programme, wearing a Wonderdog costume to promote a song made of different barks called "Ruff Mix"!

"You realise that *Top of the Pops* was the most successful as variety. People take it is a chart show but really it is a variety show."

Jan Younghusband, BBC commissioning editor for music and events

T-Rex was just one of the famous acts that promoted their records by appearing on *Top of the Pops* during the 1970s. The programme helped to increase sales for acts in the charts by showing live performances or professional dancers performing to the record.

EMI

British company EMI released records by The Beach Boys, The Beatles, The Rolling Stones, and many other famous acts. From the mid-1970s, EMI started to buy small music companies to acquire performance rights to pop and film music. By the 1990s, it was a world leader in music publishing.

Fanfare Records

In 1985, Cowell took the first step on his path to become a successful entrepreneur. He left his secure, regular job at EMI to set up his own business – a **record company** called Fanfare Records in partnership with Iain Burton, who had also been an EMI post clerk. This was a very risky move but luckily one of the first acts they signed was a female singer called Sinitta. Her record, "So Macho", was Cowell's first Top 10 hit.

Sinitta was a dancer and backing singer before Cowell helped make her a solo star. They had a close relationship that lasted 16 years.

Let others help you

Cowell had a strong belief in his own ability to spot stars but realized he didn't know everything about the business. His real skill was making use of other people's experience and knowledge to help him succeed.

Live and learn

After Sinitta's first big hit, Cowell had trouble finding another one. So he decided to bring in someone more experienced in the industry. He hired the hugely successful songwriting and record-producing trio, Stock, Aitken, and Waterman to write and help produce several hit singles for Sinitta. Fanfare also released several popular best-selling compilations of Stock, Aitken, and Waterman hits, featuring artists such as Kylie Minogue.

Stock, Aitken, and Waterman (from left to right) in front of some of their hit records. Cowell worked with Pete Waterman to learn the secrets of his success and benefit from his experience.

"I learned much over the years, from people like Pete Waterman – real tough love. He once said to me, 'You don't know what you're talking about ... Come back when you've got a hit.' I took it as a challenge."

Simon Cowell

Riches to rags

Fanfare's hits provided Cowell with his first taste of a wealthy lifestyle, but in 1989, Fanfare's **parent company** went bust. A parent company is one that pays to set up a smaller company – so when it went bust, Fanfare lost all its money, too.

Cowell with one of his luxury cars – a Bentley – in 2010. Starting in the years of his first success at Fanfare, expensive, fast cars have been one of Cowell's luxuries – it is estimated that in total they have cost over £3 million.

Although Fanfare had been doing well, Cowell had not saved any money. He had bought anything he wanted and invested heavily in **shares** that failed. He owed the bank £500,000. He had to sell his big house and his expensive Porsche car and move back into his parents' house so he could live rent-free. He claimed he spent his last £3 on a taxi ride back to his parents' house.

The right attitude

Successful entrepreneurs learn from their mistakes. Cowell's mistake taught him that in the future he would only buy something when he could afford to pay for it outright. Entrepreneurs also have to be incredibly determined and see failures merely as setbacks on the way to success.

Cowell's determination meant that he immediately began to look for a job that would get him back into the entertainment industry. Within months, the experience he'd gained running Fanfare Records had landed him a job with BMG, one of the world's biggest music companies.

> "In hindsight, it was the best thing that happened in my life because I learned the value of money: not to borrow money and not to live beyond my means. And I learned that getting there is more fun than being there. But one thing that I have always been able to do is to own up to my mistakes and not blame others."
>
> Simon Cowell

Back in business

Cowell worked for BMG as an **A&R consultant**. His job was to find new artists and new songs to create hits for BMG's pop record label, S Records. This was where Cowell's ability to spot and take advantage of current television trends first paid off.

At this time the World Wrestling Federation (WWF) was extremely popular on television, so Cowell had the idea of wrestlers releasing a single! It was a hit. Other singles linked to television series, including the Power Rangers and Teletubbies, were also hits. Robson Green and Jerome Flynn were actors on the programme *Soldier, Soldier*. Cowell made them into pop stars with the hit single "Unchained Melody" from the programme. It helped Cowell to make his first million.

In 1997, Cowell helped BMG cash in on the success of the Teletubbies by signing up the "Say Eh-Oh" single, based on the programme's theme tune. It sold over a million copies.

Tough decisions

Cowell's confidence in finding stars grew with experience. In 1998, when Irish music producer Louis Walsh showed Cowell his new boy band IOYou (later to become Westlife), Cowell was clear about what they had to do to win a record deal with S Records. He told Walsh to sack three of them because although they had great voices, they were too ugly. The three were sacked and **auditions** were held for replacements. Cowell's harsh decision seemed to be proved right when Westlife's first seven singles went straight to number one in the charts!

"I'm not that musical. I don't really know how a record is produced, and, funnily enough, I don't want to. I listen from a punter's perspective, as somebody who would buy a track. I base it on gut **instinct**."

Simon Cowell

Although it was Louis Walsh who unearthed the talents of Westlife, it was Cowell who helped turn them into the major boy band in the UK and Ireland from the late 1990s.

Cowell hits the big time

To take his business to the next level, Cowell made another bold decision – to move into television talent contests. This was a way of discovering and promoting new acts at the same time!

In 2000, Cowell turned down the job of judge on a new television programme called *Popstars*, in which singers competed to join a pop group. Cowell thought it would be a flop, but the programme became a big hit. The judge who took Cowell's place – Nigel Lythgoe – became famous as "Nasty Nigel" because of his cruel put-downs. Cowell was determined to turn his bad business decision around. He said: "I thought, 'I've got to **retaliate**.' I wanted *Popstars* off the market. I want to be on the show that's going to kick it off the air."

Both Cowell and Pete Waterman (second from left) were panellists on *Pop Idol* and their knowledgeable comments about performers, based on years of music industry experience, helped keep the viewers hooked on the series.

Launching *Pop Idol*

In 2001, Cowell got his chance. He and his friend, music manager Simon Fuller, met the head of Thames television company Alan Boyd. They convinced him that their idea for an ambitious new series to find an unknown British singing star based on viewers' votes would be a big hit. *Pop Idol* launched in 2001 with Lythgoe employed behind the scenes to help develop and produce it.

Simon Fuller (left) and Cowell, pictured here with *American Idol* winner Carrie Underwood, knew each other as fellow A&R consultants for different record labels before getting involved in television.

Simon Fuller

Simon Fuller's first big A&R success was in 1983 when he signed Madonna's first hit "Holiday" to Chrysalis Records. In 1985, at the age of 25, he started his own company and has managed stars such as The Spice Girls and S Club 7. He helped to create the *Pop Idol* television programme **format** in 1999. There are now over 100 versions worldwide.

Money spinner

As the two Simons had predicted, *Pop Idol* was a big hit. There were national auditions on a huge scale, public voting, and a live results programme. Cowell and Fuller knew that television appearances of *Pop Idol* winners could boost music sales. The winner's prize was a recording contract with S Records and artist management by Simon Fuller's company, 19. This meant that Cowell and Fuller both took a share of the profits from record sales, tickets sold for *Pop Idol* concert tours, and **merchandising**.

Cowell also gained the right to release any of the winner's future records and be the executive producer on the winner's debut album and single. This was a smart business move that earned him millions when the releases became chart successes.

Clever thinking

Cowell's good business sense ensured he made money in other ways and benefited other parts of his business through *Pop Idol*, too. In the first series, each of the final three acts recorded a cover version of Westlife's song "Evergreen", to be released by the winner after the programme's conclusion. Will Young won and his version of "Evergreen" became number one in the charts in 2002. As Westlife were signed to Cowell, the release of "Evergreen" brought him **royalties** on top of everything else – and also boosted sales of Westlife's album *World of Our Own*!

"It was the record side of it which was the primary [main] reason for getting involved, not wanting to get my ugly mug on television."

Simon Cowell talking about *Pop Idol*

All of the top three contestants from the first series of *Pop Idol*, including Will Young (above), had number one singles in the UK.

The new "Mr Nasty"

As well as dramatically boosting his record sales, Cowell's appearances on *Pop Idol* and the US spin-off *American Idol*, made him famous. In fact, many believe his appearances as a judge are what made the programme such a success. He became famous for his cruel but honest verdicts on the acts that performed in front of the judges.

Some people believe that he deliberately puts on a harsh public **persona**, especially for television. He knows that a "Mr Nasty" figure can be popular with audiences. Those who know him well claim he always had a tendency to be brutally honest. At the age of four, when he was asked if his mother looked good in a new white fur hat, he snapped: "No, she looks like a poodle!"

Cowell had his first US success with appearances on *American Idol*, starting in 2002. It was the biggest programme on US television by 2005.

Seen here with fellow judge, Paula Abdul, Cowell developed a "Mr Nasty" persona that audiences loved to hate.

Syco

Cowell realized that a lot of the money from *Pop Idol* was going to the television companies that produced the programmes. So in 2002, he created an entertainment company called Syco. The name is short for "Simon's company" – but it also sounds like "psycho" which means mad and wild. The name suggested that the company would be edgy and take risks.

Syco had two parts. Syco TV was Cowell's new television production company to create his own programmes. The other part was Syco Music, the new name for S records. It was co-owned by BMG and Cowell, so his success would earn him more.

Diversification

In business, **diversification** is when a company develops a wider range of products in order to be more successful or reduce risk. Making television programmes gave Cowell the chance to earn more, but also gave him another business in case the hit records stopped.

The *X Factor*

In 2004, Cowell created his own **reality television** series. *The X Factor*, co-produced by Syco television, is a music talent show similar to *Pop Idol*. Unlike *Idol*, the competition is open to older members of the public, not just younger performers – and also to groups, not just solo singers. Four judges act as **mentors** to the finalists, advising them on song choices and styling.

Simon Fuller claimed that *The X Factor* was a copy of the *Pop Idol* format, which he legally owned. He said that Cowell should pay him for using the format. They reached a **settlement** in 2005 in which Fuller was made a joint partner in the *The X Factor* series, and Cowell agreed to appear in at least five more series of *American Idol*.

The X Factor has been another hit for Cowell. It regularly gets half of the total viewing audience in the UK when it airs on television. Cowell made sure that his **contract** allowed him to be paid well for each programme, gave him a share of money made from the phone calls that audiences make to vote for their favourite singers, and first option on signing any of the programme's best acts to Syco Music. Artists signed by Syco Music have included international stars Leona Lewis and Alexandra Burke. In 2011, he produced and appeared on the first US series of *The X Factor*.

"Whether I'm making television shows or signing artists, you have to do it by the head and not the heart – and I run my businesses that way."

Simon Cowell

In 2011, Little Mix became the first group to win *The X Factor*.

Got Talent

Successful entrepreneurs are always thinking of new ways to increase the value of their product. Cowell re-jigged the successful television competition format to make *Got Talent*. This programme is open to all types of entertainers, from musicians and magicians, to acrobats and dog handlers! The winner receives cash and becomes the star of a live show.

Cowell knew from *The X Factor* that the public likes a mix of acts, good and bad. He launched the new programme as *America's Got Talent* in 2006 in the United States, and *Britain's Got Talent* in 2007, with Cowell as one of the three judges. It became a hit in both countries.

Susan Boyle's performances on *Britain's Got Talent* catapulted her to international stardom in April 2009. Here she is appearing on a German television programme in December of that year.

Instant star

By far the biggest star to emerge from the *Britain's Got Talent* series was Susan Boyle in 2009. Her audition of "I Dreamed a Dream" became an overnight internet sensation around the world. Within nine days it had been watched by over 100 million people on YouTube and other websites worldwide. This public interest made her first album (brought out by Syco Music) a global bestseller. Cowell was surprised by the speed that Boyle became a global star through the global reach of the internet.

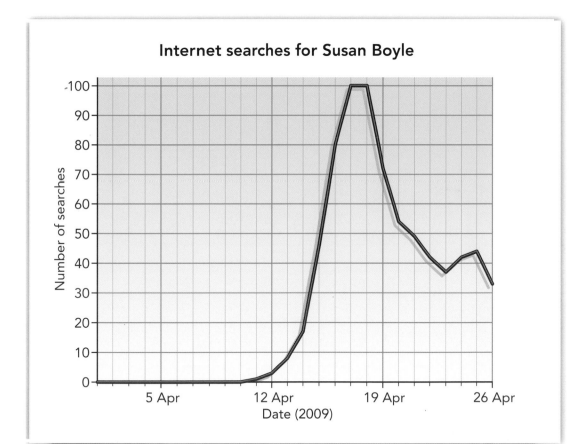

Internet searches for Susan Boyle

Records of global web searches for "Susan Boyle" during April 2009 chart the huge interest in the singer following media reviews and word-of-mouth recommendations after her *Got Talent* appearances. The graph shows the number of searches that were done for Susan Boyle compared to the total number of searches done on Google over time. The numbers are shown on a scale from 0–100.

New markets

Business people know that one way to keep **profits** rolling in is to sell the same products in more places. Susan Boyle's success and the global spread of the *Pop Idol* format for Simon Fuller convinced Cowell that there was global interest in talent shows. Syco sells **licences** to television production companies around the world, giving them permission to put on their own versions of *The X Factor* and *Got Talent*.

Cowell relied on the help of others to go global on television. For example, many Syco programmes are co-produced by FremantleMedia. This is a production company based in the UK, but with strong links to television companies in the United States and other countries. It was FremantleMedia who had meetings with US television companies and persuaded them to put *Pop Idol*, *Got Talent*, and *The X Factor* on US television.

Cowell works especially closely with FremantleMedia's chief executive Cécile Frot-Coutaz who has strong links with the big US television company Fox. This partnership benefits Syco, whose products spread far and wide – and also FremantleMedia who get paid as co-producers.

Got Talent is one of the fastest growing television **franchises**, with versions in over 30 countries.

Countries with a *Got Talent* TV programme

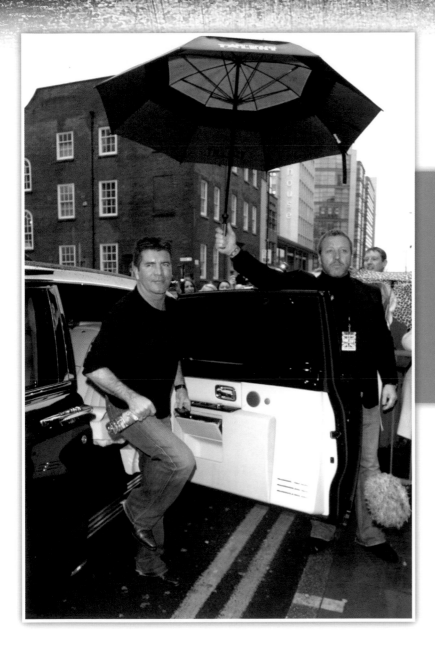

Cowell arrives at his next set of talent auditions. His future success will rely in part on whether he continues to enjoy meeting and making the entertainment stars of tomorrow.

"I think America is a hard nut to crack. But once you get a toehold it's a great place for an entrepreneur because people are so enthusiastic, and you have the most enthusiastic audiences in the world."

Simon Cowell

Maintaining success

One reason why Cowell has remained successful is that he is prepared to make changes. In 2009, after five successful seasons of the UK *The X Factor*, Cowell suddenly altered the format of the programme and filmed auditions in front of a live audience. This live approach where anything could happen kept audiences interested.

Another reason is that he creates new opportunities. For example, in 2001 he noticed public interest in light, classical-style music. So, after a long search, he found four young, attractive singers to perform in an operatic style. The group, Il Divo, went on to international success.

Il Divo's classy appeal gave them top 5 singles in 25 countries.

Move on from the failures

Most entrepreneurs have failures on their way to success. For example, in 2006 Cowell created a new US television dating series called *Cupid*. Women (such as Lisa Shannon below) auditioned men to date and won a prize if they got married. Unfortunately, audiences were so small that television networks cancelled the programme after one series, and Cowell lost money. He blamed himself for this flop because he allowed other people to make decisions about the programme's format – and also because he misread how the US public would react to a series that used marriage as entertainment.

"When you're successful you... start living in this bubble which contains your world, your shows... your staff, and your friends and you believe that's the only world that exists. That is why most successful people screw it up for themselves... because they stop listening and they stop watching."

Simon Cowell

The Cowell brand

A **brand** is not just a **logo**, like the Nike "swoosh". It also represents the special features of a business that make it stand out, such as reliability or good design. Brands can be companies, products, services, or even individuals like Cowell.

Brand identity

Cowell's brand identity is partly himself! He is well known for his abrupt personality and his wealthy, glamorous appearance and lifestyle – his tanned skin, white teeth, and smart casual clothing, and his luxury villas and fast cars. His brand also includes the things he produces. He is known the world over for producing successful popular music acts and making hugely popular television programmes. When someone mentions Simon Cowell's name, people immediately have an idea of who he is, what he does, and what he stands for.

By **promoting** himself successfully, Cowell has turned himself into a brand that people want to buy into. That means that investors are more likely to buy into his new projects and people are more likely to watch or listen to them.

USP

Simon Cowell's combination of business success, image, and the acts and material he produces have given him a unique selling point, or USP. Unique means a one-off – no one else has quite the same set of skills and qualities. Having a USP that is in demand has made Cowell a rich and famous man.

In 2011, Cowell's advert for the US version of *The X Factor* featured only him and no other judges or any of the budding pop singers. He knows people will watch the programme because they know the Cowell brand!

Cowell works extremely hard but knows he cannot do everything himself. He has a team of people to support him.

Team Cowell

The Simon Cowell brand relies heavily on the team of 32 who work at Syco. This includes managing director Sonny Takhar, branding expert Charles Garland, and George Levendis. Levendis formerly worked for the record company Sony, **marketing** artists including Beyoncé,

Cowell likes his team to be closely involved in Syco and share opinions about what the company does. For example, when Syco Music signed Susan Boyle, Cowell asked people in the office to suggest a song they would like to hear on her first album. A marketing assistant suggested the Rolling Stones' "Wild Horses", which became a massive hit for Boyle.

Cowell organizes regular meetings with critics and fans to hear their views on his programmes so he can consider changes that will make them more popular. As he says: "I work very, very hard and I expect people who work with me to do the same. I don't believe in a five-day week or an eight-hour day. I believe in 24/7."

Charles Garland

Charles Garland started work in an **advertising** agency, helping to sell brands such as Levis jeans globally. In 1998, he joined Simon Fuller's team at 19 Entertainment. He helped develop the *Pop Idol* franchise worldwide and the dance show *So You Think You Can Dance?* He also helped to build the fashion and sports brands of David and Victoria Beckham, and Skype. In 2011, Cowell encouraged Garland to join his team at Syco as Chief Operating Officer.

A caring side

Being caring towards the public is part of Cowell's business brand. He uses his television programmes not just to make money for himself, but also to help others. For example, during each season of *The X Factor*, Syco releases a single featuring the finalists. Money from sales of the single go to help Great Ormond Street Hospital for Children and Help for Heroes, a charity assisting injured soldiers and their families.

Cowell has also been involved with *American Idol*'s Idol Gives Back campaign, which has raised $140 million (£86 million) up to 2010. For every vote cast for performers, sponsors such as Coca-Cola donated money to charities.

Away from television, Cowell used his musical contacts to persuade music stars, including Westlife, Take That, and Mariah Carey, to sing a new version of "Everybody Hurts" for Syco. The recording was sold to raise money for victims of the 2010 Haiti earthquake. It sold more copies in its first week after release than any other charity single of the 21st century.

Robbie Williams was one of the stars who sang on the "Everybody Hurts" charity single.

Cowell's charities

Cowell is involved with a number of other charities. He is patron of Children's **Hospices** UK and involved in campaigning for Save the Children, the Elton John AIDS Foundation, and Help for Heroes. Cowell is also passionate about preventing cruelty to animals. For example, he appeared in an advertising campaign for the animal charity, PETA, against killing animals for their fur.

Cowell with Melissa Craven, who suffers from a rare skin condition, at the Children of Courage awards in 2003. These celebrate the achievements of children who have faced danger or coped with serious health problems.

Criticism

Some people are critical of Simon Cowell. They accuse him, Syco, and the television and radio companies that broadcast his programmes, of "dumbing down" popular music. They say that his artists are far from original and do not truly represent modern musical styles or images. Most of them simply recycle versions of old songs.

Other people say that Cowell is important for music because the profits he helps make for Sony (for instance) allow the company to invest in new musical artists.

Flooding the charts

Some artists say that Cowell prevents young talent from getting into the charts because he floods them with Syco acts, who are mostly products of his television series. Cowell's response is to say there is nothing to stop anybody promoting his or her own act.

In 2009, a Facebook campaign promoted sales of a single called "Killing in the Name" by rock/rap group Rage Against the Machine. This was done in an attempt to prevent *The X Factor* single from reaching the Christmas number one, and was a protest against the way Cowell was dominating the charts. In fact, both records were actually released on labels owned by Sony – who employ Cowell!

> "*The X Factor* is a preposterous [ridiculous] show and you have judges who have no recognizable talent apart from self-promotion, advising them what to wear and how to look."
> Sting

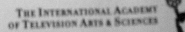

Cowell holds The Founders Award at the 2010 International Emmy Awards in New York. This recognizes his contributions to television and entertainment through his involvement in reality television programmes.

The future for Simon Cowell

Cowell only turned 50 in 2009, so he could have many years ahead of him in business. The appeal and power of the Cowell brand means that launching new television series in the UK and the United States, could make him even more successful.

The X Factor and *Got Talent* franchises continue to spread globally. Syco Music is still producing hits, and Cowell is a top television star. He is now keen to move into film. He has already created Syco Film Company and there are plans to produce a feature film about a boy band.

What next?

Will people still want to watch reality television and talent shows in the future? The reason Cowell dominates popular entertainment today is because he knows how to provide what the public want – often before they know they want it. He has adapted to changes in public taste for the past few decades, but this could change as he gets older.

Being an entrepreneur can be exhausting. Cowell has said in interviews that he almost quit in 2009 because looking at his diary he realized he had no free time for at least a year. There is no certain future in entertainment, but for now he remains a titan of business.

"If I was asked, 'Would you rather have a show seen by 3 million people and considered a masterpiece, or a show seen by 30 million people with people saying it's horrible reality television?' I'll take the ratings, thank you."

Simon Cowell

> "I'm not a master of anything. I think what I'm good at is making shows or records which a lot of people will like for the same reasons I like them. Mainly, I trust my instincts because I have very broad tastes. I genuinely believe that if I like something, other people are going to like it as well."

Simon Cowell

Cowell is a wealthy, successful man. Beverly Hills in Los Angeles, where Cowell lives, is home to many Hollywood celebrities.

How to become an entrepreneur

Simon Cowell's enthusiasm for creating pop stars led to him producing widely viewed television reality programmes that do just that. What are the things that make successful entrepreneurs, and what can we learn from Cowell's career?

Spot opportunities

Cowell looks for business opportunities in the entertainment business. He saw a gap in the popular entertainment market for his own music talent show after being involved with *Pop Idol*. He then saw the opportunity for a variety talent show along the same lines.

The right attitude

Most entrepreneurs, including Cowell, believe their failures were actually a good thing. Failures teach you how to succeed! The failure of Fanfare, plus some unsuccessful records and television flops taught Cowell how to improve his businesses.

Work at it

When asked what he considered essential for becoming a successful entrepreneur, Cowell's first words were: "Work hard." Cowell says he is available any time of the night or day to talk business.

Know your strengths

Cowell is aware of his strengths, such as his confidence, but also realizes he does not know everything about the business. For example, he has listened and learned from contacts in the music industry and television production.

Communicate

Successful entrepreneurs are skilled communicators. Cowell can be honest and critical about performers, but also about what it takes to succeed in the entertainment industry.

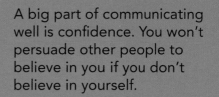

A big part of communicating well is confidence. You won't persuade other people to believe in you if you don't believe in yourself.

"Work hard, be patient, and be a sponge while learning your business. Learn how to take criticism. Follow your gut instincts and don't compromise."

Simon Cowell

Glossary

A&R stands for artists and repertoire. People in A&R work for record companies. They find new recording artists, and help them to make records and become stars.

advertising way of telling people about a product and why they might want to buy, watch, or use it

audition perform to show suitability or skill for a television programme for example

brand logo, name, and features of a business that make it special and make people recognize it

consultant person who provides professional or expert advice in a particular area

contract written or spoken agreement between people which sets out their rights and responsibilities

diversification expanding into new directions or products

entrepreneur person who takes financial risks to set up and run new businesses

executive someone who has a senior or top job within a company

film studio building where films are made

format general set-up, design, and arrangement of something

franchise formal permission given by a company to someone who wants to sell its goods or services in a particular area

hospice home providing care for people who are ill or dying. They specialize in relief of pain or discomfort, rather than cures.

instinct natural way of acting or thinking

intuitive understand something by using your feelings instead of facts

licence legal document that proves permission has been given to do something

logo symbol or image that a company uses as its special sign

marketing methods used to advertise and sell a company's products

media means by which the majority of people get news or information, including television, newspapers, internet, and radio

mentor person with experience of an industry or subject who helps and advises someone with less experience

merchandising products connected with a particular film, television series, person, or event, such as *The X-Factor* posters or mugs

nanny person employed to care for a child in his or her own home

parent company big company that owns the largest share of a smaller company

persona aspects of someone's character that they show to other people

producer person who manages a recording, television, or film project. A music producer finds a singer or band, finds a song for them to record, and promotes them.

product something that is made for other people to buy or pay for

profit money made in business by selling things

promote help sell a product or make someone or something more popular

publicity things done to get something into the media and make people aware of it

reality television programmes on television that show real people living through real situations

record company company that finds singers, or bands and songs, then records, advertises, and sells their music

retaliate make an attack or insult in return for a similar one

royalty money that is paid to someone who wrote a book, a piece of music, or a television programme each time it is sold or performed

settlement official and usually written agreement about something

shares any of the units of equal value into which a company's worth is divided and sold to raise money. People who own shares receive part of the company's profits.

suburb place where people live that is outside the centre of a city

Find out more

Books

Celeb Entrepreneurs, Laura Durman (Franklin Watts, 2011)

Entrepreneurs (21st Century Lives) Adam Sutherland (Wayland, 2010)

How to be Famous: The Ultimate Guide to Becoming a Star... , Jimmy Lee Shreeve (Orion, 2009)

Music (Behind The Scenes), Judith Anderson (Wayland, 2009)

Simon Cowell (Inspirational Lives), Debbie Foy (Wayland, 2010)

Websites

www.simoncowellonline.co.uk/

This independently run fan site has plenty of information about Cowell's life and businesses, and some good pictures.

www.fremantlemedia.com/home.aspx

Visit this website and look at the Featured brands section to discover more about *The X Factor*, *Got Talent*, and *Idol* franchises.

www.erasmus-entrepreneurs.eu/page.php?cid=2

Learn more about a European scheme to help young entrepreneurs by linking them with more established business people.

www.brightideastrust.com/our-support/case-studies/

Bright Ideas Trust is a London charity set up to help young people turn an idea into a business. Have a look at how their support has helped entrepreneurs.

www.bbc.co.uk/totp/history

Have you ever wondered what some of the music of the 70s, 80s, and 90s that appeared on *Top of the Pops* was like? Can you cope with strange haircuts, fashions, and sounds? Then visit the *Top of the Pops* website and get listening and watching!

Topics to research

After reading this book, what do you find the most interesting about Simon Cowell? What business ideas does reading about his success inspire in you? To learn more, you might want to research the following topics:

- Entrepreneurship for young people
- What a record company does
- How a television company works
- Why marketing is so important for selling products

You can visit your local library to learn more about any of these fascinating subjects.

Index

48